A Note from the Authors

Live our lives as light. In October 2001, a month after 9/11, I found myself sitting in New York City's Town Hall, listening to Arun Gandhi, grandson of Mahatma Gandhi, recount stories of his childhood. Arun spoke of living on the Sevagram ashram with his grandfather when he was twelve years old, where he stayed for two years. Arun left India to return to his home in South Africa just weeks before Gandhi was assassinated. One of the stories Arun shared that night, one of the lessons his grandfather imparted—"that anger can be like electricity"—hit me hard. It helped me heal.

A month later I e-mailed Arun and asked him to work with me on what would become this book. I had many reasons not to send the e-mail request: I'd never traveled to India, I wasn't a Gandhi scholar, I hadn't even been published yet. As unworthy as I felt, I knew from Gandhi's teachings that the *Mahatma* wouldn't see me as unworthy. Perhaps Arun wouldn't either.

Through a series of e-mail interviews, phone conversations, online research, and in-person meetings, Arun and I wrote and revised for a number of years. I had the pleasure of visiting Arun's Rochester home and meeting his beloved wife, Sunanda, before her death. Over his dining room table, while looking at pictures from his childhood, I confessed to Arun that during my childhood, my father, having been passed over for a job he felt he deserved, used racial slurs against men who looked like Arun. Arun admitted that the beatings by whites, alluded to in the text of *Grandfather Gandhi,* were only some of the prejudicial actions he suffered at the hands of those who looked like me. Our sharing helped us heal.

The world we live in needs to heal—to heal from the wars that are fought, to the bullying epidemic, to mass killings by lone gunmen, to poverty, to hunger, and to other issues that contribute to internal anger being outwardly expressed in violent actions. It is our hope, Arun's and mine, that we each look inside to see where our anger, shame, and fear hides. And when we do so, that we lovingly channel those feelings into positive action. Each time we choose to act rather than react, to sit instead of strike, to listen instead of shout, we work to create peace. We help our world heal.

Let us all learn to live our lives as light.

Bethany Hegedus and Arun Gandhi

But I did choose, and I would choose, over and over,
from that moment on, like Grandfather . . .

I did my best to live my life as light.

Grandfather slowly stood. He beckoned me to him and together we stood at the doorway of his hut looking out—at everyone working as one. He hadn't told me I was foolish. He hadn't told me I was wrong and he was right. He hadn't even forced me to choose: lightning or lamp.

. . . straight to Grandfather's hut.

"Bapuji," I cried. The same aide who had whisked Grandfather away earlier was there. "What is it, Arun?" Grandfather set down his pen and pushed aside his many papers.

It was wrong to come here. Grandfather had work to do, important work.

I backed up to leave, and Grandfather bowed. "*Namaste,*" he said—not to me, but to the aide, politely dismissing him.

A moment later we were alone.

"Tell me what has you so upset," he said.

I did. Out came what happened on the soccer field, getting pushed, the rock, everything. When I was done, my head throbbed. Grandfather didn't need to say it. I'd never live up to the *Mahatma*. I'd never be at peace.

Everyone stared—*How could he, a Gandhi,
be so easy to anger?* their eyes seemed to say.
I dropped the rock and ran . . .

After lessons, with the sun high overhead,
I was glad to head to the soccer field. I
wanted to forget about the ashram rules,
forget about being a Gandhi.

We played hard, as if the match really
mattered. I was about to make a goal when
Suman, an older boy, shoved me. His feet
stole the ball as I lurched forward and fell
facedown in the dirt. Blood trickled from
my lip. It tasted like tin.

I snatched a rock and leaped up. "You did
that on purpose!" I shouted. "Didn't you?"

Kanu stepped forward. "It was an accident,
Arun," my cousin said. "Calm down."

But I didn't want to calm down. I wanted
to throw the rock, to hit Suman, like he
hit me.

He said no more. We walked on. It wasn't long before an aide found us and escorted Grandfather away. I should have known— there were more important things than me.

The rest of the day was just as disappointing. My pencil nub shrank to almost nothing, but since we took a vow not to waste, I couldn't throw the pencil away. I held it, squishing my fingers. My hand cramped. *Stupid pencil!*

I set off after Grandfather. His stride was quick, and each time he raised his walking stick, he asked me a question. He asked about my older sister, Sita, about how Ela was behaving, and about life in South Africa and the cruelty that came with being separated by race.

Eventually Grandfather asked about me. "How are you finding life here at Sevagram?"

"The other kids tease me, and my tutor thinks I am useless," I blurted out as the path before us turned. "I try hard, but it is not enough."

I stopped short of saying that I didn't feel like a Gandhi, that peace and stillness did not come easily to me. Even Gujarati did not come easily to me!

Grandfather listened, and when I finished, he wiped his spectacles on his dhoti, put them back on, and looked me in the eye. "Give it time, Arun. You will adjust and go on to good things. I have faith."

Early in our second week Grandfather found
me. I didn't have to go looking for him.
"Will you walk with me?" he asked.

There was always some aide,
official, or follower around,
but this morning there
was no one. *Lucky me!*

That first week went by in a blur.
I saw Grandfather many times,
but for most of the day, he worked
in his hut. Whenever I'd get a
chance, I'd run a stick along the
fence post outside, waiting for some
alone time with the *Mahatma*, but
I was always shooed away. Idleness
was not allowed.

I stared at my sandaled feet. At home I spent my study time practicing John Wayne's swagger. But here at Sevagram, there would be no movies. There wasn't even electricity. No one knew who John Wayne was!

I'd tried to get the other kids to play bank robbers and sheriff, but the only game anyone was interested in was soccer, which ended up being okay. I was good at soccer, better than I was at Gujarati.

After chores it was time for lessons.
I met Bhanasalika, my tutor.
"We have much work to do," he said
upon meeting me.

Someone, maybe even Grandfather,
must have told him I didn't speak
Gujarati well.

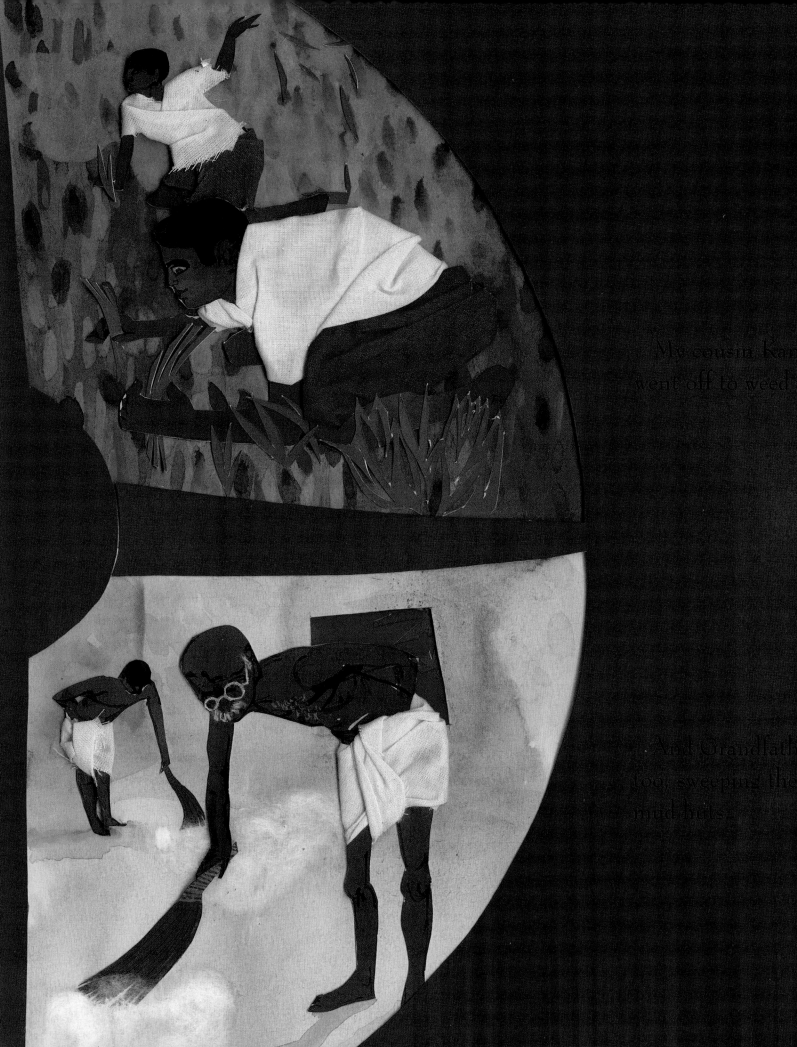

My cousin, Kanu, and I
went off to weed the garden.

And Grandfather, he worked,
too, sweeping the floors of the
mud huts.

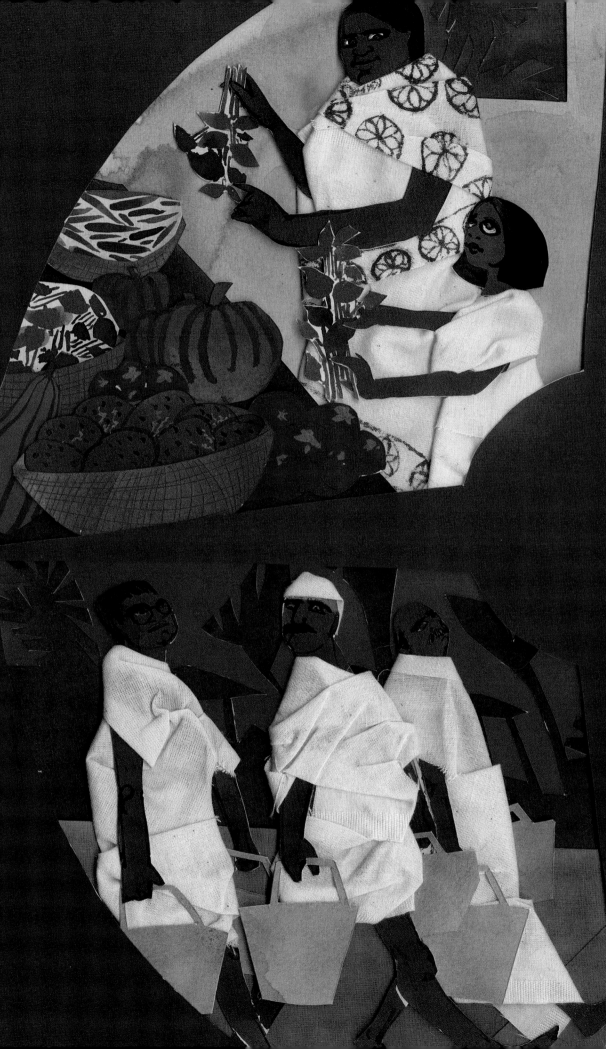

I was glad that when
the sky turned the deep
orange of a tangerine, it
was time for chores. Ela
headed off with Mother
to wash vegetables.

Father went with his
team to clean the toilet
buckets that needed to be
emptied, washed, and
put back to use.

The next day, everyone awoke at four a.m. With the dark of early morning wrapped around us, we prayed. Silence filled the air. Everyone was still, but I was fidgety. The peace of prayer felt far away.

For the rest of the night, even as I washed and readied myself for bed, my dinner sat like a lump in my stomach. The Gandhi name was much to live up to. I had passed my first test, but there would be others. What if I failed?

Mother ushered Ela and me to bed. The air was so thick and hot, we slept under the stars to keep cool. I tossed and turned, wondering what the next day would bring.

Finally I fell asleep, after even the earth seemed to quiet.

That evening I floated to
dinner. The tin bowls and
utensils we used clanged, making
a funny-sounding music. I
ate spoonful after spoonful of
boiled pumpkin. It was mushy
and bland, and I didn't like
it, but what I liked less was
sharing Grandfather. Sevagram
was filled with people. Three
hundred and fifty followers
lived here.

"Arun walked the entire way from the Wardha station," Father said.
  Grandfather stood and smiled his toothless grin. "That walk is a test of character. I am impressed."
  My heart swelled as big as a balloon. I had made Grandfather proud.

"Do you think Suman and Kanu never anger? Or that they never think injustices happen solely to them?" Grandfather wiped my tears. "Do not be ashamed, we all feel anger."

But that wasn't possible. Suman and Kanu, maybe, but not Grandfather.

"Even you?" I asked.

"Even me," said Grandfather.

Grandfather wasn't one for riddles, Father had often told me, but he was one for stories. One was coming, I was sure of it. I held the thin cotton thread between my thumb and forefinger, not moving, as Grandfather's fingers went to work.

"Have I not told you how anger is like electricity?"

I shook my head.

"It is. Anger can strike, like lightning, and split a living tree in two," he said.

I saw myself on the soccer field, rock in hand, ready to strike. I saw the movie cowboys and their guns.

"Or it can be channeled, transformed. A switch can be flipped, and it can shed light like a lamp."

I saw Grandfather, speaking before thousands. When Grandfather was angry, he didn't lash out. He worked to make changes, lasting changes, for all— not just for himself.

"Then anger can illuminate. It can turn the darkness into light," Grandfather said.

"That's what *you* do," I said quietly, sure I couldn't do the same.

"Arun, we can all work to use our anger, instead of letting it use us."

But Grandfather taught peace. I'd never seen him angry, not even now when I told him what I'd almost done.

"Let us spin," he said, and he sat before one of two spindles.

Grandfather gathered us to
him in a big hug. He smelled
of peanut oil.

We bent to touch his feet, a sign of respect.

Bapuji sat serenely on
the floor. I hung back,
afraid to be in his presence,
but Ela took my hand and
we rushed to him.

We arrived at Sevagram, Grandfather's service village, dusty and dirty.
Father insisted we be taken straight to Grandfather's hut.

December 17, 1945

Chi Arun,
I think of you every day, but
especially today during silence. Do
you spin carefully at least 160 rounds
daily? Is the yarn even? Do you
yourself fix the spinning wheel? Do you
keep a daily account? If you keep this
one promise, you will learn a lot.

Blessings to all of you from,

Bapu

𝒜
atheneum

ATHENEUM BOOKS FOR YOUNG READERS
An imprint of Simon & Schuster Children's Publishing Division
1230 Avenue of the Americas, New York, New York 10020
Text copyright © 2014 by Arun Gandhi and Bethany Hegedus
Illustrations copyright © 2014 by Evan Turk

ATHENEUM BOOKS FOR YOUNG READERS is a registered trademark of
Simon & Schuster, Inc.
Atheneum logo is a trademark of Simon & Schuster, Inc.
For information about special discounts for bulk purchases, please
contact Simon & Schuster Special Sales at 1-866-506-1949 or
business@simonandschuster.com.
The Simon & Schuster Speakers Bureau can bring authors to your
live event. For more information or to book an event, contact the
Simon & Schuster Speakers Bureau at 1-866-248-3049 or visit our
website at www.simonspeakers.com.
Book design by Ann Bobco
The text for this book is set in Bernhard Modern BT.
The illustrations for this book are rendered in watercolor, paper collage,
cotton fabric, cotton, yarn, gouache, pencil, tea, and tin foil.
Cotton hand spun on an Indian book charkha by Eileen Hallman
Manufactured in China
1113 SCP
First Edition
10 9 8 7 6 5 4 3 2 1
Library of Congress Cataloging-in-Publication Data
Gandhi, Arun.
Grandfather Gandhi / Arun Gandhi and Bethany Hegedus ;
illustrated by Evan Turk.—1st ed.
p.   cm.
ISBN 978-1-4424-2365-7 (hardcover)
ISBN 978-1-4424-5082-0 (eBook)
1. Gandhi, Mahatma, 1869–1948—Juvenile literature. 2. Gandhi,
Arun—Juvenile literature. 3. Pacifists—India—Biography—Juvenile
literature. 4. Statesmen—India—Biography—Juvenile literature.
I. Hegedus, Bethany. II. Turk, Evan, ill. III. Title.
DS481.G3G186 2012
954.03'5092—dc23
[B]   2011033058

Grandfather GANDHI

Arun Gandhi and Bethany Hegedus

illustrated by Evan Turk

A Atheneum Books for Young Readers
atheneum   New York London Toronto Sydney New Delhi